LOOKING INTO THE PAST:
PEOPLE, PLACES, AND CUSTOMS

Good Luck Symbols and Talismans

by

Thomas Bracken

Chelsea House Publishers

CHELSEA HOUSE PUBLISHERS
Editor-in-Chief Stephen Reginald
Managing Editor James D. Gallagher
Production Manager Pamela Loos
Art Director Sara Davis
Picture Editor Judy Hasday
Senior Production Editor Lisa Chippendale
Designers Takeshi Takahashi, Keith Trego

First Printing

1 3 5 7 9 8 6 4 2

Library of Congress Cataloging-in-Publication Data

Bracken, Thomas.
Good luck symbols and Talismans / by Thomas Bracken.

p. cm. — (Looking into the Past)
Includes bibliographical references and index.
Summary: A look at man's creation of and reliance on talismans, amulets, and good luck charms as a framework for life
and civilization.

ISBN 0-7910-4683-4 (hc)

1. Charms—Juvenile literature. 2. Amulets—Juvenile litera-
ture. 3. Talismans—Juvenile literature. 4. Signs and symbols—
Juvenile literature. [1. Charms. 2. Amulets. 3. Talismans. 4.
Signs and symbols.] I. Title. II. Series.
GR600.B68   1997
394—dc21   97-34377
                                        CIP
                                        AC

CONTENTS

CULTURE, CUSTOMS, AND RITUALS

The important moments of our lives—from birth through puberty, aging, and death—are made more meaningful by culture, customs, and rituals. But what is culture? The word *culture,* broadly defined, includes the way of life of an entire society. This encompasses customs, rituals, codes of manners, dress, languages, norms of behavior, and systems of beliefs. Individuals are both acted on by and react to a culture—and so generate new cultural forms and customs.

What is custom? Custom refers to accepted social practices that separate one cultural group from another. Every culture contains basic customs, often known as rites of transition or passage. These rites, or ceremonies, occur at different stages of life, from birth to death, and are sometimes religious in nature. In all cultures of the world today, a new baby is greeted and welcomed into its family through ceremony. Some ceremonies, such as the bar mitzvah, a religious initiation for teenage Jewish boys, mark the transition from childhood to adulthood. Marriage also is usually celebrated by a ritual of some sort. Death is another rite of transition. All known cultures contain beliefs about life after death, and all observe funeral rites and mourning customs.

What is a ritual? What is a rite? These terms are used interchangeably to describe a ceremony associated with a custom. The English ritual of shaking hands in greeting, for example, has become part of that culture. The washing of one's hands could be considered a ritual which helps a person achieve an accepted level of cleanliness—a requirement of the cultural beliefs that person holds.

The books in this series, *Looking into the Past: People,*

Places, and Customs, explore many of the most interesting rituals of different cultures through time. For example, did you know that in the year A.D. 1075 William the Conqueror ordered that a "Couvre feu" bell be rung at sunset in each town and city of England, as a signal to put out all fires? Because homes were made of wood and had thatched roofs, the bell served as a precaution against house fires. Today, this custom is no longer observed as it was 900 years ago, but the modern word *curfew* derives from its practice.

Another ritual that dates from centuries long past is the Japanese Samurai Festival. This colorful celebration commemorates the feats of the ancient samurai warriors who ruled the country hundreds of years ago. Japanese citizens dress in costumes, and direct descendants of warriors wear samurai swords during the festival. The making of these swords actually is a separate religious rite in itself.

Different cultures develop different customs. For example, people of different nations have developed various interesting ways to greet each other. In China 100 years ago, the ordinary salutation was a ceremonious, but not deep, bow, with the greeting "Kin t'ien ni hao ma?" (Are you well today?). During the same era, citizens of the Indian Ocean island nation Ceylon (now called Sri Lanka) greeted each other by placing their palms together with the fingers extended. When greeting a person of higher social rank, the hands were held in front of the forehead and the head was inclined.

Some symbols and rituals rooted in ancient beliefs are common to several cultures. For example, in China, Japan, and many of the countries of the East, a tortoise is a symbol of protection from black magic, while fish have represented fertility, new life, and prosperity since the beginnings of human civilization. Other ancient fertility symbols have been incorporated into religions we still practice today, and so these ancient beliefs remain a part of our civilization. A more recent belief, the legend of Santa Claus, is the story of a kind benefactor who brings gifts to the good children of the world. This story appears in the lore of nearly every nation. Each country developed its own variation on the legend and each celebrates Santa's arrival in a different way.

New rituals are being created all the time. On April 21, 1997, for example, the cremated remains of 24 people were launched into orbit around Earth on a Pegasus rocket. Included among the group whose ashes now head toward their "final frontier" are Gene Roddenberry, creator of the television series *Star Trek,* and Timothy Leary, a countercultural icon of the 1960s. Each person's remains were placed in a separate aluminum capsule engraved with the person's name and a commemorative phrase. The remains will orbit the Earth every 90 minutes for two to ten years. When the rocket does re-enter Earth's atmosphere, it will burn up with a great burst of light. This first-time ritual could become an accepted rite of passage, a custom in our culture that would supplant the current ceremonies marking the transition between life and death.

Curiosity about different customs, rites, and rituals dates back to the mercantile Greeks of classical times. Herodotus (484–425 B.C.), known as the "Father of History," described Egyptian culture. The Roman historian Tacitus (A.D. 55–117) similarly wrote a lengthy account about the customs of the "modern" European barbarians. From the Greeks to Marco Polo, from Columbus to the Pacific voyages of Captain James Cook, cultural differences have fascinated the literate world. The books in the *Looking into the Past* series collect the most interesting customs from many cultures of the past and explain their origins, meanings, and relationship to the present day.

In the future, space travel may very well provide the impetus for new cultures, customs, and rituals, which will in turn enthrall and interest the peoples of future millennia.

Fred L. Israel
The City College of the City University of New York

CONTRIBUTORS

Senior Consulting Editor FRED L. ISRAEL is an award-winning historian. He received the Scribe's Award from the American Bar Association for his work on the Chelsea House series *The Justices of the United States Supreme Court*. A specialist in early American history, he was general editor for Chelsea's *1897 Sears Roebuck Catalog*. Dr. Israel has also worked in association with Dr. Arthur M. Schlesinger, jr. on many projects, including *The History of U.S. Presidential Elections* and *The History of U.S. Political Parties*. They are currently working together on the Chelsea House series *The World 100 Years Ago*, which looks at the traditions, customs, and cultures of many nations at the turn of the century.

THOMAS BRACKEN teaches American History at the City University of New York, and has taught at Mercy College. A former recipient of a grant from the Ford Foundation to conduct independent historical research, he created a CD-ROM to be used as a review guide in conjunction with college curriculums, and has published biographies of Theodore Roosevelt, William McKinley, and Abraham Lincoln. Mr. Bracken lives in New Jersey.

The First Good Luck Charms

T alismans, amulets, and good luck charms were of great importance to the first humans. There should be little mystery why. Early man, after all, found himself threatened with many predators and natural disasters which came at him from all directions. There were great extremes of weather, shortages of food, and sicknesses which occurred for no apparent reason. And so gods were created—both angry ones who demanded forgiveness for human mistakes or offenses, or friendly ones merely seeking homage and respect. How was a man to deflect the harm angry gods might do and persuade them to bring good fortune to those he loved?

Man's direct channel to these gods whose favors he sought were the talismans and amulets he created. These, along with other superstitions and mythology, helped provide a framework for life and civilization. The exact origins of these symbols are obscure, and so we assume they go back as far as the human record itself. We can trace many of the earliest known talismans to the people of Western Asia, Egypt, and Ethiopia. The oldest known examples of these ancient good luck charms are more than 5,000 years old and were uncovered in the ancient Babylonian civilizations of Sumer and Elam, situated in what today is modern Iraq. From these ancient societies, belief in good luck charms spread to all corners of the earth.

Scholars who have studied the ancient literature of Egypt and Babylon inform us that the "magic" of these charms was believed to be an essential power of the gods.

And if the gods relied on these talismans, how could a mere mortal not?

With the progression of time and civilization, the traditions and superstitions of those primitive cultures are no longer believed. However, the appeal of these ancient good luck talismans will never be erased completely. Many people today still believe in charms or symbols they hope will bring good luck, strength, or confidence.

ABRACADABRA

he origin of the word "Abracadabra" is disputed: while some believe it is derived from the Hebrew phrase *abreq ad habra*, meaning "hurl your thunderbolt even unto death," others claim it to be a composition of the Hebrew words *Ha - Bracab - Dabarab*, which translates to "Speak or pronounce the Blessing."

What is not disputed, though, is that Serenus Sammonicus, the most learned Roman of his time and physician to the emperor Caracalla, ordered his patients to write the word in the form of an inverted cone and use it as a safeguard against all diseases.

The power of the Abracadabra to cure all sorts of diseases became quite legendary, and in medieval England one physician gained instant recognition by claiming to cure more than 200 toothaches in one year merely by placing an amulet with the word engraved on it over the necks of the afflicted people. During this period there was some dispute about the best way to use the charm. Some physicians claimed it was only necessary to repeat the word in order to cure an illness, while others claimed that a full recovery could only be achieved if the patient wrote the word on a piece of paper, chanted "Abracadabra," then swallowed the paper.

The Abracadabra was worn as a safeguard against infection during the Great Plague of 1665. The word was written on parchment and worn on a string around the neck for nine days, then the charm was thrown backward before sunrise into an eastward flowing stream or river.

ABRAXAS

he Abraxas is one of the more symbolically complex talismans that were popular in the Roman Empire after Christianity was established.

To Coptics, a group of Egyptian Christians whose philosophy also was based in part upon other religions and superstitions, God was known as Abraxas, which translates literally into "the Blessed Name." In Coptic society, he was symbolized by a figure with the head of a rooster, the body of a man, and serpents as legs, with a whip in one hand and a shield on the other arm.

The talisman Abraxas draws on the Coptic belief that God first created *Nous*, or mind, from which emanated the *Logos*, or the word, and the *Phronesis*, or intelligence, and then *Sophia*, wisdom, and finally *Dynamis*, or strength. The talisman is a combination of all five of these characteristics: the *Nous* and *Logos* are expressed by the two serpents as tokens of understanding and inner sense, the *Phonesis* is represented by the head of the rooster which said to supply foresight and vigilance, and *Sophia* and *Dynamis* are portrayed as the Shield of Wisdom and the Whip of Power, worn for protection from moral and physical illnesses.

Some scholars also believe that the ancient Hebrew equivalent of Abraxas is the palindrome *Ablanahanalba*, a loose translation of which is, "Thou art our father."

Good Luck Symbols and Talismans

ANKH

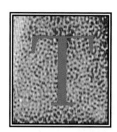

he Ankh, or *Crux Ansata*, was one of the most coveted of all talismans to ancient Egyptians. It is a combination of two hieroglyphs, and literally means "everlasting life" or the "life which cannot die."

Every god or goddess possessed one, and the ancient Egyptians believed each god's life force was maintained through his or her ankh. In Egyptian mythology, gods bestowed favors on mortals by allowing them to use their ankh. Those lucky enough to be blessed in this manner lived for "one hundred thousand millions of years," according to one legend. The ankh also held power over all evil spells.

All Egyptians believed in the power of the ankh, and many wore their own. They believed that, in addition to prolonging life, the ankh gave other gifts: wisdom, power, and wealth.

Because the Egyptians also associated one of the hieroglyphs composing the ankh with the mouth of a fish, the ankh also came to symbolize the fish of the Nile, and thus fertility and fecundity. Today, it continues to be seen on many royal emblems, and is believed to denote fertility and life.

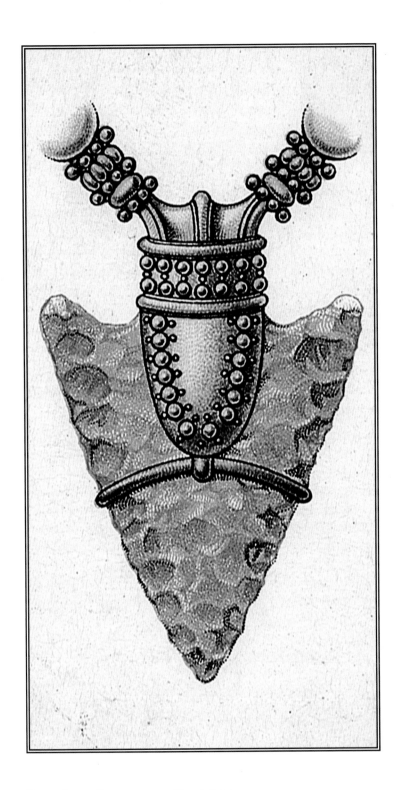

ARROWHEADS

The miraculous power of arrowheads can be traced all the way back to prehistoric times, because the men who possessed them were able to kill live game to feed their families as well as conquer the enemies of their tribe.

It is believed that Neolithic man presumed arrowheads to be charmed by the fairies, and among the magical powers attributed to them were immunity to poison, defense against the evil eye, and protection from all sorts of bodily injuries. In ancient Egypt, arrowheads were worn to provide the wearer with virility and a long family life. The perceived benefits of arrowheads varied greatly in Europe: Throughout large portions of Europe, arrow heads were used to cure cattle that had been "bewitched" by evil spirits; in Scotland, they were mounted in silver and commonly worn as charms; and in Ireland, they served as amulets against fairies and elves.

Today, modern society seems to have borrowed heavily from the Egyptian belief in the sensual powers of arrowheads. The arrowhead of Cupid is said to increase not only desire in both males and females, but also the vitality of the masculine partner in romantic encounters.

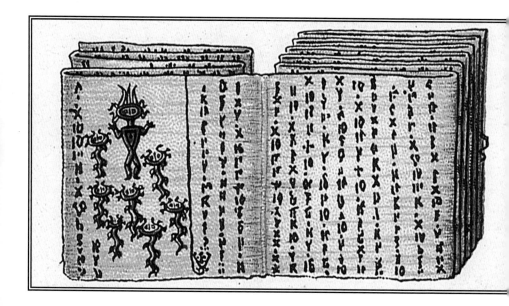

THE BOOK OF CHARMS

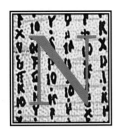atives of northern Sumatra, an island of Indonesia, practice a primitive form of religion referred to as animism. Believers claim that humans, plants, animals, and even inanimate objects possess a spirit or soul, and that these spirits are responsible for all the good or evil in the universe.

These spirits were believed to assist in healing. Tribal priests and their assistants attempted to communicate with the spirits of the dead, asking the spirits to help cure disease, which Sumatrans believed was caused by the presence of an evil spirit inside the body of the patient. Quite frequently, the names of the afflicted were changed in order to confuse the evil spirit who was causing the illness, making recovery from it far more likely.

An important element in the rituals of Sumatran life was the *Batak*, or Bark Book of Charms, which was believed to assist and advise the holy men in the administration of all their important duties. The book contained spells and incantations required to communicate with the spirits of the dead.

Still another common amulet used by the people of this island is the mounting of a bull's head on the side of their house as a way of warding off all kinds of evil spirits.

THE BUCKLE OF ISIS

The *Tjet*, or Buckle of Isis, is an Egyptian amulet which was usually made of a red substance, such as red glass or red wood, and was believed to convey the reproductive powers of the goddess Isis. In addition, Egyptians believed the buckle conferred to the wearer the strength, protection, and goodwill of Isis, and that it also unlocked mystical secrets about many other divinities. The buckle is mentioned in the Egyptian Book of the Dead:

> *The blood of Isis, the virtue of Isis, the magic power of Isis, the magic power of the Eye, are protecting this the Great one; they prevent any wrong being done to him.*

The Buckle of Isis often appears on statues and on coffins. Egyptians believed that the power of the buckle to protect them from evil spirits was eternal, and often a *Tjet* accompanied a mummy on its journey to the afterlife. The deceased, now fortified with this divine amulet, was then considered ready to enter the Judgment Hall of Osiris.

The Buckle of Isis was also a popular form of jewelry among Egyptians, and examples of them in both solid gold and gilded stone have survived.

THE CADUCEUS

he earliest known image of a caduceus appears on the design of the sacrificial cup of King Gudea of Lagash, who ruled Mesopotamia around 2600 B.C. The rod was seen as the symbol of a sympathetic god who cured all illnesses, while the entwining serpents represented fertility. The design was later adopted by the Greeks, who associated it with Hermes, the messenger of the gods. To the Greeks, the symbol combined an emblem of power (the wand) with one of wisdom (the snakes); these, when joined, came to represent healing.

The caduceus is most popularly associated with the Roman Empire. The Romans added a third element to the basic design of a rod with two serpents entwined around it— wings, which signified diligence. To Romans, the caduceus represented good moral conduct, as well as healing, and the best soldiers of the Roman legions wore helmets bearing the symbol.

In other societies, the caduceus was viewed as the integration of the four elements, with the wand representing the earth, the wings air, and the two serpents fire and water. Throughout much of Buddhist China it was regarded as a symbol of pure energy, and in India it appears engraved upon stone tablets called *Nagakals*, which are located at the entrance to religious temples.

THE CORNUCOPIA

he Roman use of the Cornucopia, or Amalthea's Horn of Plenty, as a symbol of abundance and good fortune can be traced to mythological origins. According to the story, Amalthea, the daughter of King Melissus of Crete, fed the infant Jupiter with the milk of a goat to nurse him. Jupiter grew to become King of the Gods, and as a token of his thanks, he endowed the horn of the goat with special magical powers and gave it back to Amalthea with the promise that whoever possessed it would never lack anything. In connection with its representation of abundance, the Cornucopia became a symbol of the Roman goddess Fortuna.

The Horn of Plenty also has astrological significance, as it is sometimes used as a symbol for the House of Capricorn (the Goat). This tradition is once again tied to mythology. Saturn, the Roman god of agriculture, is supposed to have introduced the science of crop cultivation and livestock breeding to Roman society.

The word cornucopia comes from the Latin *cornu copiae*, or "horn of plenty." The idea may have originated from the primitive practice of using the horns of oxen and goats as drinking cups. The Cornucopia also bears an uncanny resemblance to the *althanor*, an oven used to smelt gold—another symbol of wealth, illumination, and luck. The cornucopia charm was worn to attract good fortune.

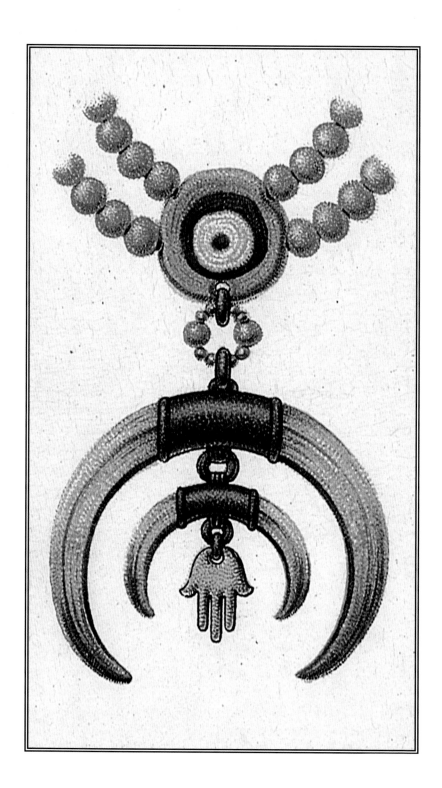

THE CRESCENT AND HAND

rescent moons, the most common symbol of the Egyptian goddess Isis, were worn by women atop their sandals to protect them from witchcraft and also to prevent the evil spirits of the moon from affecting them with lunacy, hysteria, and delusions. They were also believed to attract the goodwill of Isis, which would result in happiness—fortune in life, success in love, and motherhood.

From this charm emerged a popular regard by Greeks and Romans for the horseshoe, with its ends turned upward, as a charm against disease. This superstition continued throughout the Middle Ages; it was believed that nailing a horseshoe upon the threshold of one's house kept luck within, while preventing witches and their evil powers from entering. Additionally, it was believed that this lucky charm was especially effective if the horseshoe had been found by a member of the household.

The hand in the illustration, with the thumb and fingers outstretched, is known as the Hand of the Lady Fatima. It is still considered a powerful amulet among Muslims. Regarded as a sacred symbol representing hospitality, power, generosity, and divine providence, the fingers are said to represent the Holy Trinity, the prophet Mohammed, and the Lady Fatima. The fingers also remind Muslims to obey the five principal commandments of Islam.

THE CROSS

Perhaps the simplest, and oldest, symbol is that of the cross. This symbol was used by the people of western Asia and Europe centuries before the death of Jesus Christ. However, it is unclear if the cross was believed to possess any talismanic powers, and some scholars insist that it was used merely as a simple ornament.

The most common form of the cross used by pre-Christian peoples had four arms of equal length. This was popularized during the Kassite Dynasty of ancient Greece around 1750 B.C., and is believed to have been a tribute to the sun god that would protect its wearer against every type of evil spirit. In ancient Assyria, around 825 B.C., the four arms of the cross were believed to represent the four quarters of heaven over which the god Anu presided.

Following the crucifixion of Jesus Christ, the cross became associated with Christianity. Throughout medieval Europe, many different variations of the cross evolved. These were regarded as signs of God's protection. After the seventh century, as Islam spread, its adherents believed the cross to be a potent safeguard against sickness and witchcraft, as well as a lure for prosperity.

Christopher Columbus was amazed to find the symbol of the cross when he landed in the Americas, but in Mexican and Peruvian societies it represented the four directions of the winds and rains. In those lands, those who wore it were assumed to possess the positive characteristics of the sun. Belief in the talismanic powers of the cross still flourishes today: throughout North and South America, professional athletes bless themselves with its sign, believing it to ensure them of success in their endeavors.

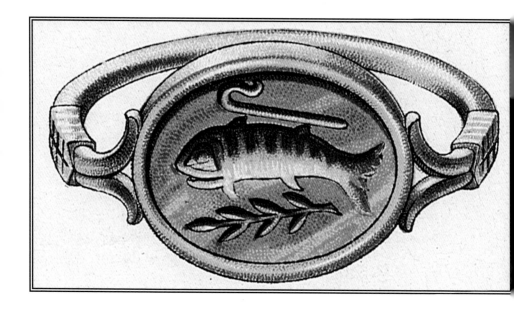

THE FISH

he fish is one of the most universally recognized of all symbols. It first appeared as a talisman in Egypt. The fish charm was a symbol of Hathor, the god who controlled the rising of the Nile, and thus was worn to secure fertility and prosperity. Because fish are depicted in the Book of the Dead as protecting the boat of Ra from evil creatures that attack it, Egyptians felt that wearing the likeness of a fish as an amulet would protect them from evil during their lifetimes. Other Egyptians believed they would be blessed with a large family by casting the talisman in gold.

Like many other sources of good luck, the charm's exact purpose varied in different areas of the world. Romans believed that fish talismans made of gold and mounted on rings were safeguards against colic and diseases, while the ancient Japanese believed that the earth was supported by a giant fish to protect it from earthquake. The Hindu use of the fish as a talisman is very similar to that of the Egyptians—proclaimed to be a symbol of the first incarnation of the god Vishnu, in India it commonly represents fertility and abundance.

Among Christians, the fish also commonly represents Jesus Christ. Two of the most popular Christian symbols of the Medieval period were the cross resting upon a fish, or a fish with a cross on either side, signifying protection from temptation, diseases, and dangers.

THE FOOD CHARM

he Tibetan reliance on charms and magic can be traced back to the 14th century, when, approximately 650 years after the introduction of Buddhism to that country, their holy scriptures were compiled into a 108-volume book called the *Kanjur*. A significant part of the *Kanjur* was devoted to *Tantra*, which the Tibetans defined as the principles which governed the use of these charms and magic, and which also delegated control of them to holy people they called Lamas.

The power attributed to the charms listed in this book is all-encompassing—Tibetans used them not only to remedy the cause of their misfortunes, but also to assure continued good luck in all their endeavors. To those who believe in them, these magical talismans can control the forces of nature and even the gods themselves. The Food Charm depicted represents the idea of the Wheel of Life, which combines birth, death, judgment, and rebirth, and is considered to be the single most important tenet of Buddhism. The food charm was used to stamp the form of the Tibetan Buddha on food. This, it was believed, would provide both happiness and protection against the powers of evil. As an amulet, the charm was, literally, a "wheel" of fortune—misfortune would roll off its wearer while good fortune rolled on, Tibetans believed.

This charm is also used to employ Buddha as a protector against all sorts of evil. Its purpose is similar to wooden "ghost traps," which were used to entangle demons or evil spirits, as well as Tibetan prayer stones, which were employed for the very same purpose.

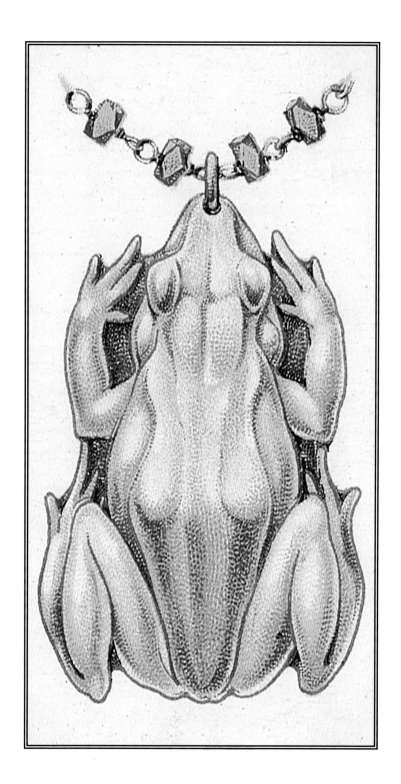

THE FROG

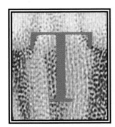

he frog was a symbol of good luck in nearly every ancient civilization. Most closely associated with the Egyptian goddess Hegt, who was believed to be present at the birth of every king of Egypt and watched all conceptions and births within the kingdom, frogs are said to be indications of fertility, abundance, and future prosperity. Because large numbers of small green frogs appear exactly two days before the Nile River rises in Egypt, ancient Egyptians regarded them as symbols of new life.

Several ancient societies, mindful of the different phases of a frog's development, adopted it as a symbol of rebirth or resurrection, and images of frogs can be seen on monuments in the catacombs of Alexandria. The physical development of frogs from tadpoles explains their common appearance on many Greek coins, where they denoted Spring, or a process of healing or regeneration. Frogs were often placed on mummies in ancient Egyptian tombs to assure a prosperous afterlife. In many central African civilizations, women ate a mixture of frogs and beetles, which they believed would ensure they would have large families with many sons.

When used as an amulet, the image of a frog is usually made of gold or hard stone, and it remains popular as modern jewelry. The frog's appeal as a talisman appears to be timeless—it is still believed to hold magical powers in some contemporary Mediterranean societies.

GROTESQUE FIGURE

rotesque figures were favored by the Romans as a type of amulet used for a decorative purpose. In addition to distorted variations of human beings, these figures often appear in the form of dogs, sheep, serpents, and an assortment of beasts.

This talisman was used by many different people of the world. The wooden figure you see was a common charm among the natives of New Guinea. These people venerated their ancestral spirits which they believed to be every-where—in the trees, in the rivers, and even in animals—and the natives believed these spirits affected human life in every way possible. Therefore, the natives were very concerned with the proper observation of customs and feast days, for if they were not observed properly the punishments would be quite serious.

The natives would often employ these grotesque figures when asking their ancestors for assistance, particularly in struggles against illness and death. Variations of these grotesque figures are also heavily relied on in the rain-making rituals of the Papua people of New Guinea.

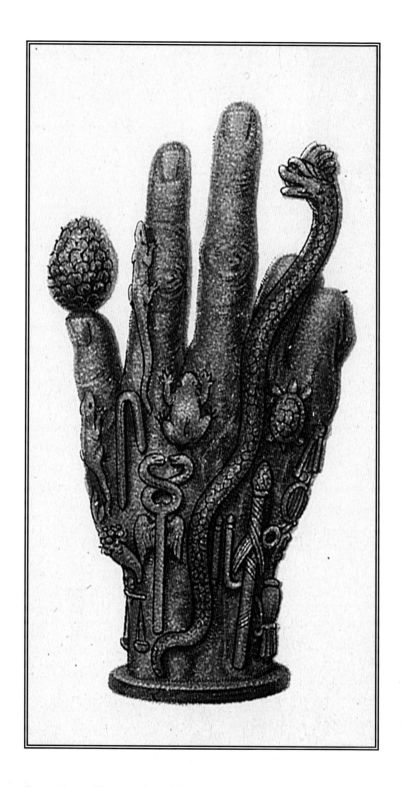

THE HAND

undreds of years ago, throughout much of Europe, the hand was believed to be a source of information about the future.

The lines on the palm and inner side of the hand were considered indications of logic and willpower, and each of the five fingers represent a particular mental or physical talent. The Mount of Jupiter, at the base of the first finger, symbolizes pride and arrogance, and the Mount of Saturn, at the base of the middle finger, symbolizes a person's fate or destiny. Other important features of the hand are the Mount of Apollo, at the base of the middle finger, from which arises one's sense of appreciation for art and music, as well as easy circumstances in life; and the Mount of Mercury, near the fourth finger, which denotes wisdom and learning. The ridges and lines on the back of the hand are said to reveal a person's general sense of character. Fingers have been credited with possessing spiritual powers in many societies.

The late Roman hand charm that is illustrated appears in the attitude of benediction (a type of blessing). Effectiveness of this charm against magic and evil was increased by the pine cone on the thumb, as well as the snake-like ring and the charms that are used to embellish the hand and wrist, the Romans believed.

Crossing the first and second fingers remains a popular rite for keeping the devil at bay even today, and the clasping of hands by strangers still serves as an indication of mutual trust and goodwill.

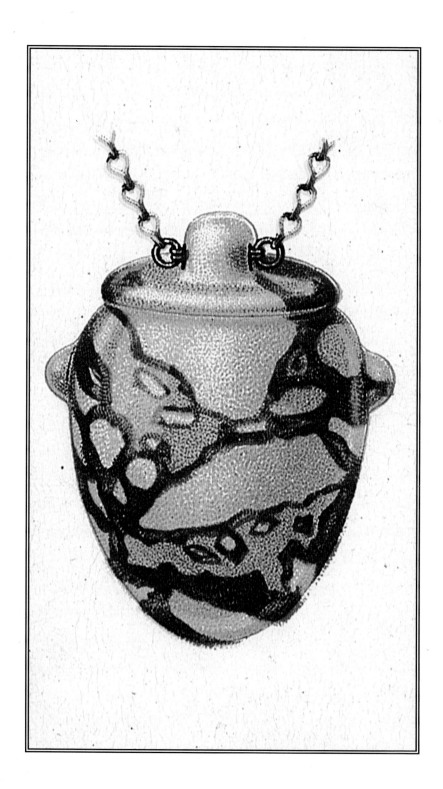

THE HEART

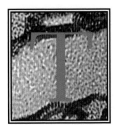

o ancient Egyptians, the heart was believed to be not only the source of all life, but also the seat of *Ba*, which is defined as "heart soul," or the soul of the physical body. The power of the unconscious mind and the secret of life were found in the heart. Because of this belief, the heart came to represent the development of a person's psychic potential.

Extreme care was taken by Egyptian priests to safeguard the hearts of the dead, and it was the priest's duty to ensure that the heart accompanied a body into the afterlife. This obligation was so sacred to the Egyptian clergy that the hearts of the dead were removed and weighed, and spells and prayers to preserve the heart are contained in the Book of the Dead.

A heart amulet cut from emerald was valued as a protection against epilepsy, and Egyptians also wore it as a charm against magicians and sorcerers. In India, the heart has served as an amulet against the evil eye, and as recently as the last century, a charm featuring a heart inscribed with a Latin cross was held in high esteem among Christians who viewed it as a powerful protection against evil.

Today, the heart is associated with human kindness: "Have a heart" is a common plea when asking someone for a favor.

THE HEI-TIKI

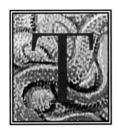

he Maoris, a native tribe of New Zealand, believe the Hei-Tiki amulet represents a long-departed ancestor. The charm is not, however, pretty to look at—with bulging eyes usually set at a 45 degree angle that are part of a noticeably tilted head, the human likeness of a Hei-Tiki is highly distorted and somewhat grotesque.

There were many purposes for the Hei-Tiki. Not only did the amulet serve as a memorial to a dead ancestor, but because it was often worn by several generations, it was believed to communicate the wisdom of these ancestors to its wearer. The Hei-Tiki is considered to possess such strong protection against evil spirits and witchcraft by Maoris that on occasion tribal wars erupted to determine possession of the amulets. Often, when a family was dying out, its last male member would leave directions that his individual Hei-Tiki should be buried with him, to prevent it from falling into the hands of other families or strangers. It then could only be exhumed by the nearest male relative of the dead person, who would then maintain the Hei-Tiki as a family heirloom.

They were usually made of a jade so rare to the natives of New Zealand that a wizard, or *tohunga*, had to be consulted to locate it. Most Hei-Tikis that survive today appear to have been made from 100 to 150 years ago. Throughout the 20th century, however, the Maoris' traditional faith in this talisman has dwindled.

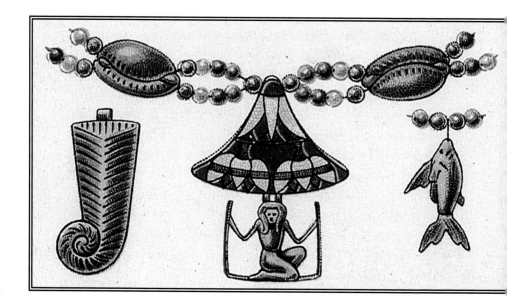

NECKLACE OF CHARMS

he Egyptians must have believed this amulet was very powerful, because it actually is a combination of three different charms believed to confer different powers: the lotus, the fish, and a lock of hair.

It is centered by the lotus. To Egyptians, the lotus was a symbol with two meanings, one of which was a designation for the goddess Isis. This became typical of purity and fertility, and was equally prized by both maidens and mothers. The lotus was also representative of the sun, and symbolized light, understanding, fruitfulness, and plenty. Egyptians believed that its use as an amulet could secure these favors from the gods. The lotus was worn as a talisman not only for good luck and beauty but also to protect children from accidents and diseases.

The fish in the illustration signifies the rising of the Nile, and is accordingly linked with fertility and prosperity. The meaning of the third pendant on the necklace, a lock of hair, is not clear. Some historians believe this charm may have denoted strength or wisdom.

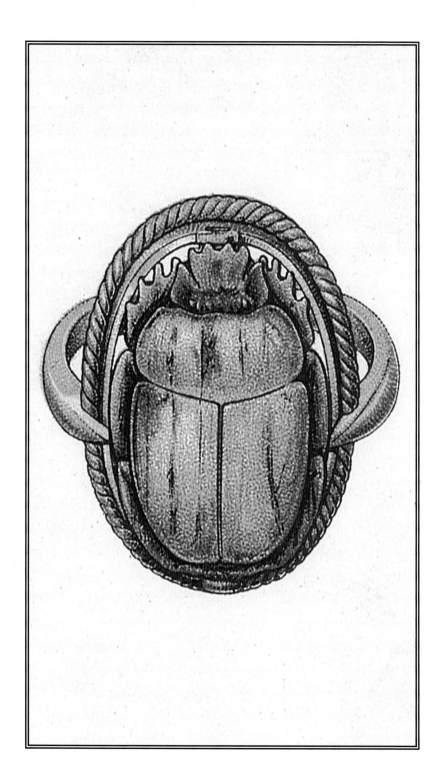

THE SCARAB

T he life of a scarab, or *scarabaeus sacer*, is not a particularly glamorous one, but from it has emerged one of the most universally recognized talismans ever. This beetle lays one egg in a mass of dung, which it then rolls into a ball. When the egg hatches, the tiny beetle grows and flourishes. Out of this simple process of birth and rebirth the Egyptians constructed a spiritually complex system of values, and scarabs became not only symbols of creation but also of the renewal of life after death.

Scarab amulets were made of nearly every kind of material, and varied in length from half an inch to two inches. The Egyptians often placed scarabs in the tombs of their dead, as they did with frogs, to ensure a happy afterlife. Scarab charms also served as gifts between Egyptian friends, and frequently came engraved with inscriptions such as "May your house flourish every day!" or "May your name be established, may you have a son."

Scarabs have also been used as amulets in Assyria, Babylonia, and Phonecia, where they embodied the virtues of fortitude and eternal life as early as 4600 B.C. Particularly in Babylonia, the charms assumed an almost mystical identity. Today, scholars believe that Mediterrean societies ceased to believe in them as sources of good luck sometime around 550 B.C.

THE SERPENT

 lthough serpents are represented as evil in the Bible, many other ancient peoples considered serpents a sign of good fortune. Because it sheds its skin, the serpent was considered by ancient Persians the most spiritual of all animals, and symbolized to them the concept of resurrection. It almost always appeared on the headdresses of Egyptian royalty, and was thought to be an indication of the wisdom, energy, and divine power of the king. To Greeks the serpent represented the concept of healing; to Romans, long life and vitality.

But the talismanic appeal of the serpent was not limited to the Mediterranean countries. In many other societies, the serpent is believed to represent health, longevity, and wisdom. In Great Britain, the dried skin of a snake was believed to not only protect a house from fire but also bring good fortune to the family living in it. In India, serpents were thought to be the guardians of life and immortality, and also of the superior riches of the soul that are symbolized by hidden treasures. As ornaments on rings in India, snakes were believed to ensure strength, health, and long life to those who wore them.

THE SEVEN GREEK VOWELS

he seven Greek vowels are found in a variety of combinations on amulets, usually in the form of a triangle. Each line is not allowed to contain more than seven characters, and deep mystical powers are attributed to each particular letter. Each of the vowels represents a planet, and collectively the vowels symbolize the seven heavens.

According to tradition, each of the seven vowels has seven different sounds, with each one of them corresponding to a certain universal benefit, such as good health, happiness, wisdom, fortune, or foresight. The benefits of the talisman are realized when the wearer correctly utters each of the 49 sounds correctly.

The charm of the seven vowels usually appears in the form of a triangle. The mystic significance of this type of arrangement dates to ancient Egypt, where this form was thought to supply the wearer with virility, prosperity, and health. As this tradition evolved in Egyptian society, it became more closely associated with medicine.

Among the more curious uses of the seven Greek vowels is the Greek belief in the charm as a protection against seizures, and the belief that if the vowels were set in stone and tied to a person's chest, mouth, or stomach, the charm would benefit these areas of the body.

SOLOMON'S SEAL

olomon was regarded as a great and wise philosopher-king by the Hebrews, and his seal, featuring the six-pointed Star of David, is easily recognizable. The two triangles that compose the star have different meanings—the upward triangle represents the virtues of truth and wisdom as well as the more earthly elements of fire, creation, and spirit, and the triangle pointing downward is equated with the vices of falsehood and folly in addition to water, destruction, and the material world. The phrase "Go forth thou, and all the people who are in thy train" has been discovered engraved in different varieties of the seal that were used as amulets by the Hebrews. The seal was so powerful that the ancient Hebrews even believed it capable of performing miracles.

A version of Solomon's Seal was found drawn on pots discovered on ancient Babylonian sites. On this charm, the seven discs represent either Babylonian kings or divinities. Variations of this amulet also appear in India, where the two triangles represent the gods Siva and Brahma. Hindus regarded this figure as defining the essence of a virtuous life. Among the more curious talismanic powers attributed to the seal over time are protections against the ravages of fire and against back pain.

THE TAU CROSS

lso called St. Anthony's Cross, the Tau cross is commonly found in the catacombs of Rome, and was worn by ancients to protect them from snake bites and diseases. Authorities believe the Tau cross was originally used as a talisman representing power or authority by primitive man. This was probably because of the Tau cross' resemblance to the ax, one of man's earliest tools.

Throughout antiquity, extraordinary significance has been placed upon this particular talisman. In many religions, the form of a cross was regarded as the symbol of eternal life, and Christians believe the death of Jesus Christ on a cross gives spiritual life and immortality to all mankind. The Tau cross was popular as a cure for epilepsy among both Hebrews and Egyptians, and it was later used to denote the presence at roll-call of those Roman soldiers who had survived a battle.

The Tau cross was a visible relic of the Order of St. Anthony in the Middle Ages. This group's primary mission was to comfort those afflicted with *erysipelas*, an inflammatory affection of the skin. The Tau cross also was used in Ireland as a talisman against sickness.

Its primitive use as an emblem of authority still survives today in the form of the gavel or mallet, which is wielded by judges as a tangible reminder of their influential status.

THE TORTOISE

Although green slate statuettes of tortoises or turtles were used as amulets for unknown purposes in Egypt as far back as the Neolithic period, the most popular use of a tortoise talisman was in ancient China, Japan, and India. In these countries, the tortoise was regarded as a symbol representing the Universe. Its cone-shaped back represents the vault of the sky, while its belly is said to equal the earth that moves upon the waters.

As tortoises usually enjoy long life spans, wearing the charm is believed to bring longevity. In addition, because of its protective shell, the tortoise is viewed as a symbol of strength and endurance. Throughout much of Eastern Asia, the Tortoise was relied upon as an effective repellent of both black magic and the evil eye, as well as a symbol for good luck. In Greek or Roman art, the Goddesses of Love, Aphrodite and Venus, were frequently linked to the Tortoise.

Belief in the Tortoise as a lure for good fortune became so powerful and so popular that it eventually spread from Asia to such distant countries as Portugal, where tortoises, along with lizards, are often affixed to the exterior walls of houses to attract good luck, long life, and prosperity.

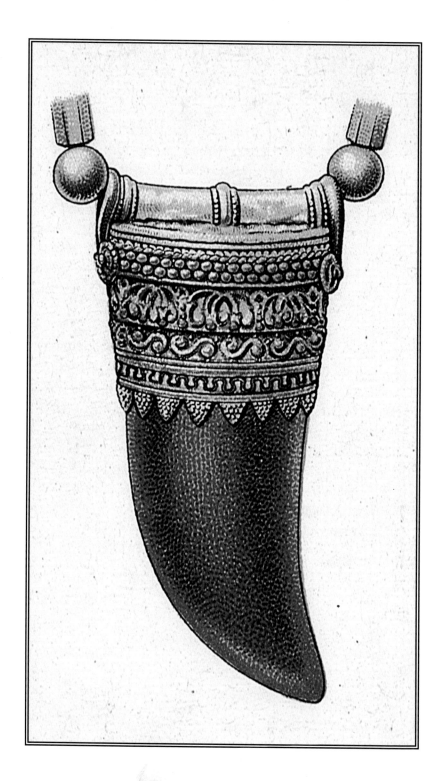

The Tusk

he tusk charm was very significant to ancient Egyptians because of the deep reverence they felt toward Isis, who as a goddess represented many things: the earth and all its bounties; the sea; the Nile River; and love, magic, and healing. As the Tusk became synonymous with this powerful goddess, the Egyptians came to believe the charm would bring long life, fertility, and protection from many forms of diseases, in addition to many other benefits.

Other civilizations also used animal teeth as amulets. The Roman writer Pliny noted that a tooth, particularly that of a wolf, was a very potent talisman for children, especially if they hung it around their neck. This would protect them from infections of the teeth and gums. The Roman charm pictured at left is carved from basalt and mounted in gold.

And, curiously, the Tusk emerged in other lands as a good-luck charm for gamblers. In China, the tooth of a tiger was considered a valued ally in all games of chance, and a badger's tooth, if worn from the right-hand pocket of a waistcoat, was believed to be a common talisman for luck at card games in many societies.

CHRONOLOGY

4,600 B.C. Scarab charms were believed to bring their wearer good fortune and long life in Assyria, Babylonia, and Phonecia

3,110 B.C. Tortoise, cross, and frog charms were used by Egyptians seeking good luck and prosperity

2,600 B.C. The earliest known image of a caduceus appears on the design of the sacrificial cup of King Gudea of Lagash (Mesopotamia)

2258 B.C. During this obscure time in Egyptian history, archaeologists believe charms such as the Buckle of Isis and the Necklace of Charms were first worn

1,750 B.C. The cross is popularized by the Kassite Dynasty of ancient Greece as a tribute to the sun god. It was used to protect its wearer against every type of evil spirit

922 B.C. Hebrew King Solomon dies in Jerusalem

825 B.C. The cross is used in Assyrian society. Its four arms were believed to represent the four quarters of heaven over which the god Anu presided

290 B.C. Following Alexander the Great's conquest of Egypt in 332 B.C., talismans containing the seven Greek vowels begin to appear in Egypt. These were used for healing and to provide good fortune

67 B.C. The cornucopia, or "horn of plenty," becomes a popular symbol for the Romans around this time

A.D. 1400 Tibetan Buddhist priests compile the 108-volume *Kanjur,* which outlines the tenents of the religion. One section is devoted to *Tantra,* the principles governing the use of charms and talismans

1511 Portugese explorers visit Indonesia and learn about native customs. Among their discoveries are the Sumatran Book of Charms, which contained spells and incantations the native priests required to communicate with spirits

1850 Belief in the Hei-Tiki amulet by the Maoris, a native tribe of New Zealand, begins to wane

Index ♣

FURTHER READING

Alderman, Clifford Lindsey. *Symbols of Magic: Amulets and Talismans*. New York: J. Messner, 1977.

Bonner, Campbell. *Studies in Magical Amulets, chiefly Graeco-Egyptian*. Ann Arbor: University of Michigan Press, 1950.

Budge, E. A. Wallis. *Amulets and Talismans*. New Hyde Park, N.Y.: University Books, 1992.

Farrone, Christopher A. *Talismans and Trojan Horses: Guardian Statues in Ancient Greek Myth and Ritual*. New York: Oxford University Press, 1992.

Jones, William. *Credulities Past and Present*. Detroit: Singing Tree Press, 1993.

King, Charles William. *The Gnostics and Their Remains, Ancient and Medieval*. London: Bell and Daldy, 1864.

Kunz, George Frederick. *The Magic of Jewels and Charms*. Philadelphia: J. B. Lippincott Company, 1950.

Lockhart, John Gilbert. *Curses, Luck, and Talismans*. Detroit: Singing Tree Press, 1971.

Pavitt, William Thomas. *The Book of Talismans, Amulets, and Zodiacal Gems*. Philadelphia: D. McKay, 1914.